9-12-09.

Karen,
God's Peace,
Bernadette J Meyer

Halfway Home
The First 50 Years

She Who Writes Her Own Story
(A collection of random stories and an interactive journal)

Bernadette A. Moyer

This book is not only about my friends, mentors and life experiences it is meant to be much more. My hope for its readers is that it triggers within you the desire to share and write your experiences. In doing so, I hope you come to the place where I have arrived of deep abiding love and gratitude for all I have experienced, happy and sad, in my first 50 years.

Cover photograph by Joy Crimmins

Halfway Home

ISBN Library of Congress Catalog Card Number 978-0-9666183-0-3

All proceeds from the sale of this book will benefit The Monsignor O'Dwyer Retreat House Capital Campaign for The Founder's Youth Recreational Facility. Located in Northern Baltimore County in Maryland and currently serving over 8,000 young people annually. Retreat house programs are rooted in the Catholic tradition for grades 8th – 12th. For more information, visit www.msgrodwyer.org or bmoyer@archbalt.org or bmoyer37@aol.com or www.facebook.com/bernadette.moyer

Thank you …

Sally Bowen

Joy Crimmins

Carole Gibison

Tina Gonglewski

Rev. Martin Nocchi

Dr. Andrew Ross

Brian Sahm

Brandon Sahm

Briana Sahm

Suzanne Singleton

Teresa Wilkins

Mary Wodka

Thank you God for my life!

August, 2009

Dear Friends,

As I come to the conclusion of this book project, so many thoughts and feelings are circling around me. It has been about a year since the conception of this project and I am still writing some final stories. The hardest story for me to write would be the last one I would write, yet there was a place for it from the very beginning. It is the one about my mother. The mother is the one person who is supposed to love us no matter what we do. My story with my mother also draws down to my story with my daughter. What behavior did I unknowingly model that would later turn in on me.

Relationships can be so tricky, even the best ones will test us from time to time. Maybe the worst ones are where we learn the most valued lessons. Every one of us has a story; I am no different than anyone reading this. We have all experienced many things in our lives. Later this year I will celebrate my 50th birthday and yet I still marvel at life and the fact that each one of us has a unique life path. How wonderful life is!

I have witnessed laughing out loud, as my stories have been read and I have been told, "You have overcome a lot." I never lived my life as a victim; my thoughts are you are only a victim if you choose to be one. I have however been tested and come out a stronger person. I am thankful for the riches of all my life lessons.

A Priest friend has a homily that I like and in it he says, "You are only as sick as your secrets." The older I am the more open I become and the healthier and whole I feel. During the writing process I was determined, and now that I am about to finish I am filled with excitement and honestly some fear. I have opened myself up, I have put myself out there and with that will come comments and criticism. I know.

Please enjoy my stories and I sincerely hope they will help you to write, and reflect on the riches of your own life stories.

God's Peace and Angel Hugs,

Bernadette A. Meyer.

5

Table of Contents

On writing

I am a published author of both books and articles and this is all I am going to say about writing.

It is my belief that writer's fall into one of two categories: they are either very good story tellers or they have a story to tell. I fall into the second category. I know many people who are much better writers than I will ever be, but I also know I have shared stories where people have connected to me through tears and laughter. I write for the connectedness which I crave with others, and I write for my own therapy and hope that in sharing I am helping someone else. I am a strong believer in writing for therapy, writing for art and plain old diary and journal writing.

I have learned, there is "no such thing as writing, there is only re-writing." There has yet to be anything I have had published I haven't looked at later and thought I could have edited to make it better.

In my writing projects, the challenges for me include my jumping off point and then staying with it. I write to make it right.

Do you write, or wish you could? What do you enjoy writing?

If you think you can, you can!

This was the mantra from my middle school when I was in the sixth grade and one I still follow. If you think you can, you can! If you believe it, it will happen.

In my mid-20's I was the youngest real estate agent in my office, working in a high end office on a street I refer to as the "land of good and plenty." It was a street lined with high end private schools and residential wealth. Not only were the agents older than me but wealthier, some lived in multi-million dollar homes. At the time I was renting an apartment for a few hundred dollars. I had been renting apartments as a manager when an older than I, friend and mentor stopped by to visit. I had taken the apartment complex from 72% occupancy to 96% occupancy in a few months. When I shared this he said, "You really should go into real estate sales, that's where the money is." So I did.

I studied hard, received my license and my first year sold 12 units to exceed a million dollars in sales. Immediately I was in the top 20% of the agents in my office. Most all were better connected, had more money and prestige. What I had was attitude. I knew I could so I did. I lasted 10 years and in the first two years purchased my first home by myself. It was a great job for a single mom raising a child. I could drive my child to and from school everyday. Real estate was good to us, within those first few years, I not only purchased a home but afforded private school for my daughter and bought a new car.

I worked hard for my success, but the core of me was all about, if I knew I could, I would, and I did.

Twelve years ago I decided to write a children's book about death, a close friend's husband laughed and said, "Yeah right." Years later I learned when their family priest came to bless their new home he pulled out my book to share. Generally I don't say things unless I believe it to be true.

Words are powerful, if you tell yourself you can, you will! If you think you can, you can!

What did you think you could accomplish that no one else really believed when deep down, you knew your drive was greater than the challenge?

Volunteer work

My mother raised us to believe that "idle time is a devil's workshop!" We were always encouraged to "do something." As a child I was out from sun up to sun down. Even before I began working for pay I worked full-time as a volunteer. I loved it; I felt important. My life had value. I learned early that by helping others I was helping myself.

The summer I was 13 was one of the best summers of my life. I was trained as a volunteer candy striper and worked for Sacred Heart Hospital in Allentown, PA. I loved that job! I wore the pink and white striped uniform, white cotton blouse, white shoes and white hose with the little matching cap. I delivered the mail and flowers to the different patient's rooms. For many this was the highlight of their day; they were always happy to see me as I delivered cards, notes and gifts. I loved stopping by the nursery to check on the newborn babies, and on to the kids in the pediatric unit. I was trained to administer C.P.R. and how to make hospital corners in bed making. I helped out wherever I was asked, and was paid in "thank you" and anything I wanted to eat for lunch from the hospital cafeteria. Like most jobs when you become good at them, they want to promote you.

Promotion for me meant moving to the wards with sick people, ending in the recovery room assisting nurses in transporting patients from surgery to the recovery room. I saw many things there. I witnessed a friend have tonsils removed, and a man who had his leg amputated. It was eye opening for a young girl.

During this summer I worked at two camps as a volunteer, I was a C.I. T. (Counselor in Training) for a YMCA based day camp and spent two weeks at a Girl's Club resident camp. The day camp was up early and catching the bus to the YMCA and then off to the campsite. As a C.I.T it was my job to support both the Counselor and Unit Leader. Eventually I was trained to teach swimming and archery. The day camp included all kinds of activities and was my introduction into resident camp.

Once I started in resident camp over the next four or five years, I moved from C.I.T to Counselor and ultimately ended up as a Unit Leader. I loved camp. The first week was with kids who came from families that could afford many experiences for their children. We hiked, swam, played games, made arts & crafts, sang and sat around huge bon fires.

The second week was sponsored by the Police Athletic League; the P.A. L. kids were a huge challenge most came from underprivileged families. I had kids in my cabin that did drugs, sniffed glue and exchanged sex for compensation. These kids were tough. You couldn't pacify them. You needed to bring your "A" game. There was no fooling them. The biggest difference from the first group to the P.A. L. kids, the P.A.L. kids didn't want to be there. Yet these were the kids who touched my heart. I gave them my dolls, stuffed animals, and hair ribbons. I kept up with a few of them for years after, taking them to lunch or the library and I would shop for them. If you were authentic and could get through their barriers of self-protection, these kids connected with you. When I left for school I wrote letters and called them. They were always so happy to hear from me. When I came home and met with them, they brought all the notes, letters and cards I had sent. It surprised me to see my tattered letters. They had saved and valued them. It didn't take long for me to understand all they really wanted was attention, love, care and concern.

Do you volunteer? If so, how does it enrich your life?

You only need to get fired once

When I was 16, my mother talked me into working at a nursing home for the elderly; they used to call them convalescent homes. At that time you didn't need certification and I was trained on the job to be a nurse's aid. The pay was just over $2 an hour. The drive was about 15 minutes from our farm and the convalescent home located in a country setting. The people there were at the end of their lives. Many days I would show up to find that someone had passed away during the night. Others were strapped in jerry chairs and had to be fed like a child. I recall a man that walked the halls constantly snapping his fingers for his dog, "Sammy" to follow along. (There was no dog!)

Another woman sat on the front porch and rocked, she told me she was waiting for her daughter to visit. Her daughter never came. A married couple shared a room and dressed with their jewelry, fine attire and wigs. At night we helped ready them for bed by removing their jewelry, switching out their day clothes to sleepwear and removing their wigs.

Cleaning out bed pans and changing bed sheets was a large part of my duties. Each day I showed up in my white uniform and I always arrived upbeat. Seldom did it last – I hated that job! It takes a certain kind of person to work with the sick and elderly and it just was not me.

One rainy day driving to work I had a car accident and blew out the car radiator in my Ford Pinto. I called out from work, and took a few days off before I returned.

On the day I returned to work, the owner, my boss asked to see me. He told me they were regulated by the state and they needed me to be there when I was on the schedule. He told me he was letting me go, I was fired! It stung like any rejection but deep down I was thankful. I hated that job. Within days I recovered, and was hired as a sales clerk in a department store. I loved my new job, I started as Christmas help but did such a good job they kept me on.

I learned you can only be truly great at the work you do if you love it! And you only need to get fired once.

Have you ever worked a job that you knew was not for you? Have you ever been let go, fired?

My Mother

The mother is the one person who is supposed to love you no matter what. I was told that my mother almost bled to death after I was born and that they sent me home and kept my mother in the hospital. This may have set the tone for our relationship. I was the second daughter and my parents were hoping for a boy.

Growing up my mother and I were never really close, my four sisters were much needier than me. I favored my father or he favored me. I am told my mother was thin and tall and had saved herself for marriage. My father had a reputation as a ladies man. My parents lived on the same street in Lansford, Pennsylvania. She came from the right side of the tracks, he didn't. She was Italian Catholic, he was Irish Catholic. Her father never approved of my father.

My mom quit nursing school to marry and would later return to become a registered nurse and years later would receive her master's degree. She was very intelligent and probably should have been a doctor.

When my parents divorced I was just pre-teen and blamed my mother. At the end of their marriage she was twice her size, and had become, "I am women hear me roar" career driven.

She was not feminine, and our relationship was void of any meaningful interactions. She was closest to all four of my sisters. When my first husband died I was so humbled that I forgave everything. It was a clean fresh start. During this time I acknowledged that I had moved past a point in both my parent's lives as I was now widowed with a child. This was the closest Mom and I ever became. She was good to my daughter and we shared many weekly lunches. This was also the period when my mother met her second husband. I was thrilled that she finally had someone special to share her life with. I was the only daughter to attend the wedding, though none of us were invited.

The only real heart to heart recall I have is that I told my mother I was sorry for any upset I may have caused her. I never wanted to be a burden. Her response to me was, "you were easy, you never asked for anything." Then I had this light bulb moment. I watched my mother work double shifts to keep our home and raise five daughters. I watched my sisters constantly going after her for what they wanted. I was so afraid that if I asked for anything it would be the one that sent her over the edge. So I learned to take care of myself.

The final test in our relationship would be my daughter; she confided in me that my mother's husband was abusing her. My mother didn't want to believe it and stood by her husband instead of us. After this I had years of anger toward my mother. I felt like she wasn't there when I was growing up and now she wasn't going to be there for my daughter. Years ago I forgave her so I could disconnect. After the abuse allegations came out, we never had any relationship.

I am thankful that I was never put in this position, but I have thought about it. My mother decided to "stand by her man" she and I never related again. The hurt would come from my feelings that she should have loved us and wanted a relationship with us. She didn't. After that, for me, I would never take my children around a known abuser. This decision may have cost me my daughter, as it was modeled behavior for her. She didn't grow up to see a healthy mother-daughter relationship.

What gifts does your Mother have? What gifts do you wish that she would have had?

Daddy's Little Girl

I was my father's daughter, his namesake by default as he was hoping for a boy. I was born the second oldest. My sister was three years older and my parents would go on to have three more daughters. My sisters were all "girly girls" and I was a tomboy. Like my dad I dressed in jeans and a jean jacket and I preferred his jeep to cooking in the kitchen with my mother and sisters. My dad was cool! Mom seemed more matronly.

Like all kids I learned to manipulate and one of my favorite stories still makes me chuckle. Our family was visiting with family friends who had six children. The kids were expected to play together and the adults were gathered around the kitchen table. I was probably in my early teens. I was that kid that enjoyed adult conversations. I never spoke but like a sponge took it all in. Adults seemed so much more interesting to me. Many times that day I was told, "Go play with the other kids."

Throughout the day the kids were playing games and watching movies. Finally I found a way. The kids had started to play spin the bottle, first I was like yuck! And then I was out of there. I went to the kitchen and quietly stood over my father's shoulder. After a few minutes almost in unison my parents said, "Why don't you go play with the other kids?" I said, "Dad, they are playing spin the bottle." His response, "you stay right here." My mother wasn't happy but the entire rest of the night I was with the adults and loving it.

My dad always took up for me which only added to the great divide. Not long after my parents divorced, I found myself without an ally. I blamed my mother for the divorce and for my father leaving. In my eyes at that time he could do no wrong. Clearly I would grow up to change that opinion, as it was my father who left his marriage when he found someone new.

What was your relationship like with your father?

My God

As a young girl I was born and raised Catholic, probably around my teenage years I began to question my "force fed faith." We were expected to be "good Catholic girls" no questions asked. Not sure if it is my personality but I have come to believe that "force feeding" anyone anything especially when they may not be hungry is probably not the best approach. It certainly was not for me.

I grew up with Catholic Nuns as my teachers and was told that regardless you would never achieve a 100% on your work because "God was perfect and you certainly were not God nor perfect." I was also led to believe that we were all going to hell. So yes there came a day when I questioned my faith, was it mine? Or was it someone else's imposed upon me?

I can say that I have always been a spiritual person, I have known a spiritual strength most all of my life. When widowed and riddled with guilt after my first husband passed, it was God who gave me strength to move on. It was God at 3:30 in the morning when I was crying my heart out who held me safe and helped me to make it through the cold of the night. When my daughter was hurt and we lost my family once again it was God, the Catholic Church, the daily treks to the beach and my writing that sustained me for the year we moved away to Ft. Lauderdale, Florida.

The only time I gave up on God was just after my oldest daughter left my life. My rationale was you can take anything from me, have it all, but no God, not her! I was bitter and past hurt and anger. I wanted to cease. It was the first time that I quit on my faith, there was no peace. It was also the first time that I requested medication. I couldn't make it on my own. I needed therapy and I needed anti-depressants. I couldn't find or see My God. I truly felt abandoned.

This period in my life was foggy and full of sleepless nights. Often I started in my bed and would move to one of the twin's beds and rest awhile before I would retire to the couch and then our guest room. It was common for me to have attempted sleep in four to five locations during the course of one night. I was constantly searching and looking for my daughter or any sign that she had been around. I looked for her everywhere.

I have come to believe that for me, faith is vital; many times in my life it has sustained me. But I also believe that just because I am Catholic, that we are not all right and all other faiths are wrong. I believe that faith is a personal thing and that it is between me and God. I know that God had his hand on my back as he gently guided me to my job with the Archdiocese of Baltimore. I know that only God could bring me back without a fight. I started work on All Saint's Day and had the honor of celebrating mass with three others in the chapel at the O'Dwyer Retreat House. When mass concluded I rushed off to my office and closed my door, the tears that had been bottled up rushed right through me. God had brought me back like only he could, without a fight, without a public display, without humiliation.

23

I work with people that have studied theology and the bible in great detail; I have witnessed some of the best and some of the worst in my faith. I have come to believe that yes there is a God and that each one of us will come to know him in our own way. For me, it is My God.

Do you have faith? Do you have a relationship with God? How do you feel about religion?

Prayer

I still pray like a child! Every night before I go to sleep I pray the same prayer that I learned as a small child.

It goes …

Now I lay me down to sleep
I pray the Lord my soul to keep
If I should die before I wake
I pray the Lord my soul to take

Years ago I wrote my own poem/prayer;

A Child's Prayer

God, I am whispering
A soft whisper to you
Please hear me
I really want you to
You see I need you
To be my friend
Perhaps, I have been naughty
My ways, I am sure to mend
Mostly I am lonely
And cold inside and sad
Please could you come and help me
Really I would be so glad

Now child I am whispering
A soft whisper to you
Please hear me
I really want you to
You see I need you
To be my friend
I will send my love to help you
So try and make amends
Yes you have been lonesome
Soon to go away
For I will never leave you
I am here with you to stay

Do you have a favorite prayer? Could you write one?

Conservation before it became cool

My grandparents were raising seven children during the great depression; they came to this country from L'Aquila, Italy. They came with nothing but a desire to build a better life. They believed in hard work and education.

My grandmother understood conservation long before it became trendy or cool. She had a hundred ways to re-use the plastic bag that came with the loaf of bread and one hundred and one ways to re-use the twisty tie closure.

They believed in hard work and Sunday was a day of rest. My grandfather worked in the coal mines by day and worked in their bar and hotel at night. He was a brick layer, stone mason, hunter and fisherman. He kept hunting dogs, made wine from grapes and planted a garden. I can remember visiting the hotel and stumbling into a huge bin that contained the fish he had caught. I remember going into the hotel basement and seeing a deer hanging upside down with the blood draining out waiting for him to butcher. He was a big man with a solid conviction on how to live his life and care for his family. He spoke fluent Italian and learned to speak English. In the late sixties he would suffer from black lung disease that would take his life. A strong independent man humbled by illness. I remember being afraid of him. He spoke his mind and he spoke it clearly. I also remember when he was dying how soft he became. I remember sharing my coloring books with him and how artistic he was. He colored in circles and it was just beautiful. He wasn't afraid and lived a full life. His seven children would achieve through education and go on to be a doctor, teachers to a nurse and several successful businessmen. They would also go on to have twenty-seven grandchildren.

My grandmother was half his size and just as spirited. She could make something out of nothing. With a bag of flour and a bag of sugar and a few random ingredients she created homemade pasta dishes, cakes and cookies and the best pizza. In owning and running a hotel she was a cook, cleaning lady, business woman and entertainer. She was the matriarch of the family. Although she never completed high school, she was one of the wisest women I have ever known. She planted and cared for a garden, she ironed bed sheets, she cooked and she cleaned for her family and the hotel they owned. She knitted and was always up on current events. Every person that crossed her path, she wanted to learn more about.

They believed in God and in this country, they believed in saving for a rainy day. My grandparents never wasted anything and they understood the value of hard work and education.

What lessons did you learn from your grandparents?

Take the time to be alone

Women, I believe have a much more difficult time spending time alone and going out alone. Even as a teenager I would enjoy walking downtown to Allentown to shop and browse the stores. We lived in a neighborhood where you could walk to school, church, the stores and to the bakery, the library and to the movie theater. Long before I was driving a car I walked everywhere. At times I would go out with my girlfriends and many time I ventured out alone. I loved exploring places and having the ability to move about at my own pace.

When I learned to drive a car I enjoyed going places both with my friends and alone. As I evolved I would challenge myself to go out on my own. I have taken long road trips from Maryland to Florida alone. The drive was a declaration of independence and also the best thinking time. Moreover, I'd enjoy a movie or maybe out for a meal. It is my belief that to learn who you are you have to have experiences on your own. You have to be willing to spend time alone with yourself both in a crowd and completely alone.

By nature I am a very social person I absolutely love spending time with my family and friends. This past Sunday was a simple pleasure as I enjoyed most of my best friends at our church pancake breakfast. It was a perfect way to enjoy a part of our Sunday morning. When I spend time with my friends and their husbands and kids I feel refreshed. I am reminded as we share stories that we are more alike than not. I am reminded that I am not alone.

I have also learned to love my "me" time as I am writing this story in a beachside coffee shop at a table by myself. For the next few days I am writing which I love. And I am practicing self care. Self care for me is a simple as purchasing fresh fruits and cutting them up into a big pretty bowl. Every time I open my refrigerator I have a bright healthy choice looking back at me. I have pineapple and cantaloupe and blueberries. I went tanning at the salon for instant relaxation and will have a manicure and pedicure. I am bike riding and I am walking on the beach, I am window shopping. I am listening to music and I am enjoying quiet moments.

Earlier today I spoke with a close friend, we are the same age. She asked me, "don't you mind being alone at your beach house?" No! That was the whole purpose of this particular trip. There will be many times here at the beach where we will come as a family and other times that we will entertain our friends. This time is about me as I explore my surrounding and again reacquaint myself with - me!

Taking time to be with me, it refreshes my heart and my soul and I believe it makes me a better wife, mother, friend and co-worker.

Where do you go alone? How do you spend time with just – you?

What no one knows

During my 20's I was in an abusive relationship. I was with a man who forced himself sexually on me, and hit me in the face with a clenched fist. I stayed longer than a woman should have. There was only one reason I stayed. I stayed to prove everyone else wrong. My friends and my family and the family priest all saw what I chose to deny. This man was not a good person, and he certainly was not good for me.

However, that was not what I wanted to hear or believe. I'd show them. I would change him! The first time he forced himself on me, I was too proud to tell anyone. I didn't want to be wrong and everyone else to be right. I cried all afternoon and night. The next day we had plans to show a friend from college some local hotspots. We went to a rose garden and walked around looking at flowers and the lily pond. I had swollen eyes from crying so much and wore sun glasses the entire day. My feelings were numb. I wasn't strong enough to end it or even speak out. My friend took many photographs. Weeks later when she shared her "beautiful" photos of the gardens, all I could see was my pain the morning after I had been so hurt.

The next time it happened, I called the police. When they came, all I could muster up was, "If you don't leave, I will tell them what you did to me." Still protecting him? This time I went home and told my mother. She listened but did not offer me a safe haven. My sense was she felt, "You've made your bed, now lie in it."

I felt rejected by my mother and went back to him. Things didn't get better and as time passed, I grew to dislike him immensely. I planned my departure for months by saving money and securing my own place. On the day I told him it was over between us, he clenched his fist and hit me in my face. I fell down and skidded into the corner of the room, covering my face he grabbed me by the front of my shirt to pull me up on my feet and push me around even more. It was over! I left and never looked back. Any love that I may have had for him was completely gone.

My guess is that people who know me today would be shocked by this story. I am a strong woman and yet I allowed a man to abuse me. I was conflicted on whether to share this, but believe others may benefit. The woman I am today would never tolerate this in any relationship. In my 20's I wasn't secure or strong enough. After I went to therapy and grew in my accomplishments, I learned I deserved better.

Was there ever a time when you felt abused by someone? How did it feel? What did you do to save yourself?

This Strong Woman

(Dedicated to all women, who struggle as I do, in maintaining our femininity, yet, still aspiring and developing our strength!)

This strong woman
By chance and not by choice
Tested and re-invested
To the ground, on my knees

This strong woman
I resent her so
She takes my femaleness
Then cries out my name

This strong woman
Chartered and weathered
From humbled beginnings
To limitless skies

This strong woman
Still so soft
An unprotected heart
Finding, her own blood stay

This strong woman
Hurling back
Day after day
Moving toward her sights

This strong woman
Resented by some
Yet loved by most

This strong woman
Bridled young, and
Yet, not bridled none

Can you write a poem that describes you?

Regret – the hardest pill to swallow

I don't know many people who don't have their share of regret. We have all said and done things that we could now cringe over. For me, I have learned that the line, "you did the best you could with what you had at that time" helps me to move past my regrets.

In parenting it is easy to have a certain amount of regret. Things you look back upon and know you would do differently later. One of the lessons I learned in working with teenagers is, never ask a question you are not prepared to hear the answer to. I remember asking a teenager, "are you having sex?' The response was honest and I was not prepared for the answer. I handled it horribly. The small inner voice was telling me "stay calm", "bite your tongue" "do not overact!" And what do you think I did? I completely blew it – big time! So I have learned never ask a question that you are not prepared to hear the answer to!"

In a general sense the only other regrets I have are the things I didn't stay with, follow through with or maybe try just a bit harder to achieve.

In a relationship or marriage, in my youth I may have been looking for perfection in someone that was different to fill my own voids. Later in life I would come to know there is no perfection but each person comes with their own "stuff" and you could change partners but what you get is someone new with different "stuff," issues that they bring.

When my first husband died I remember thinking I would rather do something, say something than look back later and regret that I didn't. I do my best to live my life so I won't have to swallow the regret pill!

Do you have regrets? What are they? What could you have done differently?

Jealousy

As a young girl, I had my share of jealousy. That awful feeling that someone has something you believe you should have. It could be a relationship, a career, an outfit, car, wealth or any other perceived measure of value.

I still witness women both younger and older than I, who allow jealousy to show itself. Remember when it used to matter more how many people attended your party? Now I can honestly say it is the quality of the people that means the most to me. Do they have a good heart? Do they possess a healthy spirit? Do they have a positive outlook on life? Are they happy? Will I learn something from the relationship or will I have an opportunity to teach something?

When I sold real estate I remember many highly successful agents who were openly angered when they didn't get to list a certain house. Somehow in their minds all the business belonged to them. Even back in those days I was always happy when one of my associates sold a house or garnered that well sought after listing. I used to tell myself, "Good for them and now it is one time closer to my turn."

I learned how to be the same way back when I was in the restaurant business. A lot younger at that time often my friends would be making what sounded like fun weekend party plans. I had to work most weekends and holidays. I can't tell you how many Mother's days, Christmas Eve's, Thanksgivings and New Years I once worked. But that was when you made your money and when you were most needed. So I finally learned how to psych myself up for work, I would tell myself I was going to a party and I was the hostess. With this attitude I made a lot of money and while most of my friends were out drinking and spending money I was in a fun environment and I was making money.

If we create the life that we want to live, there is no reason for jealousy.

Was there a time when you were jealous? What was it that caused you to feel that way?

On giving birth

She was born just three days after my 21st birthday and I felt like the football player who made the touchdown that won the game! My entire family was there. Both of my parents worked in the small Catholic hospital where she was born. My father worked in the engineering office and my mother was a supervisor nurse in the intensive units. My older sister was an inhalation therapist and they were all there waiting on the birth of the first grandchild. My husband and I had been married a few months short of two years and our daughter was both planned and desired.

Best advice I received came from my mother, even though I was married and we had been trying to conceive, once I found out I was pregnant fear set in. She said, "You don't just wake up one day ready, you go with it and when the time comes you will find that you are ready."

My labor was long, more than 22 hours and it was and still is to this day the most physical pain I have ever endured. I will never forget the pain nor will I forget the joy. In many ways it was the happiest day of my life. My daughter was born healthy at 8 pounds 1 ounce and she was 21 and half inches tall. Her father picked her up just moments after her birth.

I have vivid recall of that day. She was born 10/10/80 at 2:41 in the afternoon. Her head was full of dark hair and she took to breast feeding easily. From the very beginning she was a good and content baby. I never knew this kind of love before. The purest form where you give and you give and you expect nothing in return. In a way it made me question all my other relationships.

Within three weeks she was baptized at St Thomas More wearing the most beautiful handmade knitted christening outfit that my grandmother had made and given to me at my baby shower. Recently I had it preserved and framed. For me it represents both my first born but also the generations from great-grandmother to daughter.

Celebrate your children's lives for as long as you have them!

Share the story of the birth of your children here?

I love you bigger than the sky times two

My love for my children has always been "bigger than the sky times two" I have always wanted my children to know they were conceived from love, and were wanted long before their conception.

It is easy to love a good kid. Some of the best parental advice I have ever received came from a successful movie producer, James Robinson, more than 26 years ago. He said, "Kids, when they deserve your love the least is when they need your love the most."

I grew up during a time when children had a healthy respect for parents and adults. "Children were to be seen and not heard." My sisters and I grew up knowing where the boundaries were, and the consequences of our actions. We knew our parents loved us and were doing the best they could. We trusted that they were older, lived longer, and knew more.

Today's kids seem so different. Generally I sense a lack of fear and respect. They seem angrier and inept at handing life's curve balls. Lately I have heard multiple stories in the news where teenagers have killed their own parents. The most recent shocking story came out of Canada where a father had taken away an Xbox video game from his teenage son and the kid committed suicide.

Recently a friend said her son pitched a fit, after getting his drivers license and learning the newly purchased family car was not for him. It reminded me of a time when we pulled all the extras like HBO from our cable service and had weeping children. You would have thought we took food off the table. We were cutting back but what struck me was how spoiled our kids had become.

"A parent's job is to give a child what they need not what they want." from a social worker friend.

I have and always will love my children bigger than the sky times two.

What have your children meant to you, the significance of your children in your life?

From the mouths of babes

We were strolling around the Inner Harbor in Baltimore City on a warm August day back in 1983. We were in one of the food court areas just me and my beautiful two year old daughter. She points to a man that neither one of us had ever met. She loudly proclaims, "what about him?" "What about him?" I question and she responds, "Yeah for a husband for you!" Her father had passed away just a few months earlier.

Didn't see that one coming but how sweet and a tiny peak inside of her 2 year old mind!

On another day my little girl lost her helium balloon and I seemed more upset than she was. Her calm quiet response was, "that's ok it is going up to heaven for my daddy."

Our son has said more than a few things that caused us a good belly laugh, like the time I was drinking a diet 7up and he asked if he could have some of my zup.

Recently our youngest daughter was filling out a job application, and there was a part toward the end that asked, "Is there anything else you would like to tell us before we consider you for hire." Her response was. "I go away a lot."

Around this same I told my son that next year we should start looking at colleges, his response, "I think I'll wait till I get through high school before I worry about that."

Think about what gems came from the mouths of your children?

Daddy died, leaving a wife and daughter

In retrospect, I was often uncomfortable in the normal school atmosphere with peer parents. My daughter always attended private Catholic schools and I was acutely aware that I was a single mom. My husband died when she was only 2 years old. We were different, but it was not by choice. I wondered if I was a bit defensive about it and whether I unknowingly passed on my own feelings of parenting and family inadequacy to my daughter.

There were many school functions, plays and programs where the two allotted seats went to the parent, and in the beginning I went and sat next to "the empty seat, "where her father should have been. "The empty seat" that would have and should have been shared by the only other person who would fully understand the pride I had known with our daughter.

After a few years of this, I stopped going to these functions altogether and found other ways to celebrate with my daughter. This was my attempt to move away from "the empty seat." Again, years later, I wonder if perhaps these actions may have led to some anti-social or self-esteem issues. Of course, I could not see the harm in it at that time.

I believe that my daughter never really understood the loss of her dad or death until her senior year in high school. That year, one of her close classmates unexpectedly died. This brought to the surface so many feelings my daughter had yet to deal with: grief, rage, and anger. These were characteristics that previously never described her.

She had one foot already headed out the door. Colleges had accepted her, she was working part-time, and her boyfriend took up a lot of her time. Somehow my influence was diminished.

We did not have the normal mother-daughter struggles that are really a natural progression to independence. I believe she would say I loved her and worked hard to keep it all together and going. I also believe she tried to keep the water calm, even to her own detriment. The biggest problem was the type of boyfriends she would attract: boys who were consistently less intelligent and motivated than she was.

We had counseling and some family support. As a surviving parent and mother of a child, I would later learn just how easy I was to manipulate. I have read that all children test and manipulate to one degree or another. However, a surviving spouse with a child is an easy target for manipulation. You will feel sorry for your child, you will try and make up for this tremendous loss, but in the end that it's the worst thing you can do. Talk to your child, cry with your child, grieve with your child and remember that crying never hurt anyone. This too shall pass, and as with any rainstorm, the sun will shine all the brighter when the rain has gone.

(Originally published Sept 2001 in *Surviving Ophelia* (Mothers Share Their Wisdom in Navigating the Tumultuous Teenage Years) by Cheryl Dellasega Ph. D.)

Share your thoughts

My Friend Mary

Mary and I met while working together in the restaurant business. We were both in our early twenties and both waitresses. She was not someone that I was immediately drawn to. She seemed standoffish and a bit snobby. During breaks she was always off in a corner reading a book. Mary had expensive gold jewelry and designer shoes and I was a struggling single mother. Our worlds seemed very different and very far apart.

Then one night Mary and a male co-worker asked me to join them for a soft crab sandwich. Apparently it was the season! Born and raised in northeast Pennsylvania I had not known of or ever eaten a soft crab sandwich. So I happily agreed to join them. But … when I saw those crab legs hanging over the sides of the bread? I took my obligatory first bite. Just one bite and that was it for me and soft crab sandwiches. I have however become very fond of hard crabs and old bay seasoning!

Time and work schedules would throw Mary and me together as we often had the same days off. One night our friendship really started, we had gone out with a group from work Mary included and we went to a neighborhood bar. The music was loud we were all burning off steam from a frantic work day and drinking fairly heavily. Mary and I had a great time and yes we were drunk. That night Mary asked me to drive her car that we both arrived in, as if I was in any better shape than she was! Her car was a stick shift and I just couldn't manage it. We were literally a mile or so from both our apartments. I couldn't drive and neither could she, so we got out of her car and sat in a grass field on a warm balmy summer night.

The Mary I knew was reserved and now it looked like the cork was coming out of the bottle. We sat there and Mary told me her life story. It was jaw dropping and heart breaking. Out of respect for her privacy it is not my story to share. But what I can say is that night our friendship truly began and the bonds have now lasted 26 years. In these 26 years Mary has been my best friend, at times my mother, my sister and always a source of strength!

Everyone needs a friend like Mary. We have fought, we have reconciled and I am better for all of it. Mary is one of 12 kids; I suspect she has deeper knowledge in getting along than I with so many siblings.

Who is one of your best friends? What can you share about him or her?

"Everything ends badly or it wouldn't end at all." Tom Cruise in the movie Cocktails

Now it seems obvious to me after having been widowed so young, I would turn to a younger man. Michael was five years younger than me, he was fun and reckless. This was the only time in my life; I was involved with someone who I loved more than he loved me. When a man says to you, "I see how other men look at you and you have never done that for me." you really should question yourself.

Michael was tall and intelligent and so much fun, these were the things that I loved. He also was without a plan, had little direction and truthfully hadn't yet found himself. I turned away better men, I know.

The relationship lasted just over five years and was the nastiest breakup; it absolutely brought out the worst in me. He went to work one night and decided to go off with a new co-worker. The next day he couldn't look me in the eye and refused to discuss it. Without words, he took his key and placed it on the table. This translated to, it was over between us. I never had the chance to have any input; he had decided alone that "we" no longer existed. He was having an intimate relationship with a girl he barely knew. I would later learn that she and I had a few mutual friends and acquaintances, I felt like I was naked on main street and the whole world was watching.

My relationship was with Michael yet I wanted to go after her. He was the one who stepped out of the relationship yet it was easier at that time for me to blame her.

This happened the same year when I learned my daughter was abused and I had lost all my family support. I was already furious with my mother and now I had this break up to deal with. I was working as an independent contractor selling houses and had a daughter who was really hurting. The bottom fell out.

I decided we needed to get away and sold our home and moved to sunny south Florida. During that year we became whole again. My daughter was enrolled in a new Catholic school and became active in a toastmasters club. When I dropped her off in the mornings my routine was to go to church and then sit on the beach and write and pray and cry it all out. When she came home we rode bikes, took long walks on the beach and talked. She was such a bright wonderful girl. She was my whole heart.

Several months passed when Michael called, he wanted to come down and reconcile. We did for a very short time and ended the relationship in peace and dignity this time. I no longer wanted it. Later we would meet throughout the years as friends until we both married.

Looking back my past relationships continue to help me appreciate all that I have right now. On occasion my husband Brian will say to me, "wouldn't it have been nice if we would have met in high school and started our relationship then?" I always respond the same, "we wouldn't have been ready for each other."

I believe we needed to learn and to grow from all our previous relationships before we could fully commit and appreciate what we now share.

There is so much growth that happens during a break up, I am just thankful that Michael and I could come together later and end it appropriately with peace.

Have you had a break up that you learned from? What lessons did you learn?

Girls just wanna have fun!

My friend Suzanne invited me and my daughter to her Florida beach home to spend time with her and her two children. We enjoyed the beach and swimming for a few days. After the third day, Suzanne and I took a break from the kids to go to lunch and enjoy some shopping.

Leaving the kids with her son's girlfriend, off we drove 40 minutes to the small quaint town of Dunedin, full of eateries, boutique shopping, and bars. It was a bright and sunny day and we were chatty. The lunch was a perfect ladies lunch. Once finished we noticed the adjoining bar. It was a martini bar with what seemed like at least a 100 choices of flavored martinis, everything from green apple to lemon to watermelon and vanilla and more. Looking back it seems we may have tried most of them!

It was daylight, yet the bar was dark, and I recall, had just a few patrons. We had two, possibly three martinis as we sat talking on the bar stools. The time just flew by and we paid our check. When we got up to leave we realized we were tipsy. We knew that driving was completely out of the question.

So opening the doors to the bar, our faces were hit by the burning Florida sunshine. There is something so wicked about a daylight buzz from alcohol consumption. We decided to walk it off and ventured into a few boutiques to browse. My cell phone rang, it was my husband. All I said was, "Hello?" My husband responded "Are you drunk?" I was so busted!

Green apple martinis continue to be one of my favorite drinks! And Suzanne is always at the top of my list for times when girls just wanna have fun!

Green Apple Martini Recipe

Equal parts green apple pucker liquor and vodka (choose a good quality like Grey Goose, Absolute or Sky) I prefer the shaker method. Shake well.

Rim glass with sugar cinnamon mixture or twirl caramel sauce in glass
Float a thin slice of green apple in the martini Enjoy!

Which one of your friends makes you just wanna have fun? What experiences have you enjoyed together?

Everyone needs a Tina

My friend Tina is my cheerleader friend, the one who always thinks I am amazing. Tina is younger than me, and always very positive. I have said before, it takes a lot of really good girlfriends to have a long and happy marriage. Tina and I talk: her troubles, my troubles; we share.

Some people have a knack of just being there. She is that person. In the early 90's I moved to Ft. Lauderdale, Florida. I was away from friends; and my family had gone bust after the abuse allegations. That Christmas was lacking for me. First I had no friends and family but also the weather was different from the north, with the cold temperatures and snow. It was warm and balmy in Florida. I was alone. I walked from my car to my apartment and was overcome with tears. I put the key in the door, looked down, and found a package. Tina had sent me a Christmas gift! It was music, classic Sinatra, and I danced the night away listening to it.

When I visited Baltimore, Tina was always one of the friends who seemed happiest to see me; it was reciprocal. Years later, after I had moved back to Baltimore, Tina worked part-time in my retail store. I appreciated her organizational skills and talents. That job and our relationship helped get her through post-divorce.

Recently another friend said to me, "Tina thinks you are amazing, that you are perfect and do no wrong." My response "what's wrong with that? Everyone needs a Tina." I pray I never fall from the pedestal she has created for me!

Do you have a good friend who is your very own cheerleader?

So we were going to a fat farm in Connecticut, ended up in Ft. Lauderdale

It was March in the mid-1980's, and my friend Mary and I took off for a week at a "fat farm" to try and lose ten pounds. We had booked the trip through a well known weight loss center and excitedly drove to Connecticut. Neither of us had ever been to this kind of place.

We were greeted by two women who seemed different from what we had expected. We were taken to our rooms and left alone to get settled. One quick glance around and together we said, "I can't stay here!" The place was not at all spa like but rather worn down and dirty. I didn't want to put my hand on the bed let alone sleep in it.

Mary was the driver so my fate was in her hands, when she said "let's go!" Before long we were in route to the Newark airport and moments later boarding People's Express airlines to Palm Beach Florida. Oh the days of People's Express, you could arrive at the airport jump on a plane and pay once in the air.

Here we were with suitcases full of winter clothes and now headed to a tropical climate. The first few days we stayed with Mary's sister before going off on our own to Ft. Lauderdale. We cut off our pants to make shorts and the arms off our sweatshirts. Thank goodness it was the era of "Flashdance" and this look was the style. We purchased some flip flops and were set.

We sat on the beach; talked, visited with friends, shopped and enjoyed the night life. We had a blast. The trip was such fun and so spontaneous. We arrived back in Baltimore on St. Patrick's Day and met friends and co-workers at an Irish pub. They couldn't understand how we managed to get such great looking tans during the winter week in Connecticut.

Did you ever start out going to one place, and ended up in an even better one?

I found my husband, by *not* dating

Some people have a natural ability to date; it is as though they go to the smorgasbord and have the ability to try some of this and some of that, me I was never good with dating. I was meant to be married. I was the person who showed up at the buffet line and looked over the offerings and was like no, not that, hmm, I don't think so and then, ah, yes, maybe that one!

Even as a young woman I would rather spend time alone than be in the company of someone that I was not fond of. Yet I have had many close friends who loved dating, were very good at it and loved to flirt. I love being married. I enjoy knowing I have someone who cares for me and loves me, I like knowing who my date is on Saturday night. I enjoy really knowing someone not just the façade put on for first dates. I was that terrible date, who when I just didn't feel it, wanted to go home. I have left dates at dinner and at parties, no I am not proud of it. I never wanted to hurt anyone's feelings, but I always had this feeling inside that if it wasn't right for me – it just wasn't right.

I applaud those who date and enjoy it. I am just not that person. I am meant to be married. The year I met my second husband, I had given up on dating. I had friends who were all trying to fix me up, I went out with my share of lawyers, doctors and the last date was with a dentist. That was it for me. It was a fix up through a friend, this guy was ready he wanted marriage and kids and he wanted it yesterday. During our first date while driving home he showed me the neighborhood where "our house" would be? This guy barely knew me! I received an amazing amount of flowers the next day. I was so scared I just threw up my hands and gave up on dating.

I decided I was doing well on my own, I had a thriving real-estate career, good friends and my daughter was in private Catholic school. She was the love of my life. I was saving money and looking for a new house and most probably a convertible car. What the heck, it was going to be just her and me and I decided my focus would be career and kid.

On Good Friday in 1992 I was asked to baby-sit for my realtor friend's grandbabies. Her daughter had died and left behind pre-mature new born infant twins, a boy and a girl. I was introduced to their father while I was holding his tiny daughter. I couldn't take my eyes off of him. He looked just like Richard Dean Anderson from the series MacGyver and the soap opera General Hospital. I loved that guy! But I also knew this was the first time I was meeting someone even close to my age who was widowed and left with children. Brian and I would become fast friends, it didn't take long until we discovered we were both Italian, both Catholic and both came from large families. We were also both born in 1959 and he had married the twin's mother on my 30th birthday.

One of our earliest dates would be me cooking dinner for him. When he arrived he was holding 2 baby baskets, they were the car seat carriers. The twins were dressed in matching boy and girl sailor suits and smelled from fresh baby powder. Brian was clean shaven in a pressed shirt and jeans, it was obvious he had put much time and care into preparing the twins and himself for our dinner. While most men bring flowers and chocolates, here was this man on my steps with baby baskets filled with twin babies! How could I not lose my heart to all of them?

I had given up on dating and I was living my life doing the things I would just naturally do and along came my husband. So, *not* dating has worked out for me.

Did you or do you enjoy dating? Recall a special date?

My husband Brian

One day while driving in the car my husband Brian asked, "Is this working out for you?" I was unsure as to what he meant and I guess the look on my face expressed it. He pointed to me and then himself and said, "This" I responded "our marriage?" and he nodded.

I let out a nervous laugh. Where was this coming from after 17 years of being together? "Yes!" I said, "Of course – why?" As my friend he wanted to know if I was happy, and getting what I needed from our relationship. Women tend to push for these moments. I never saw it coming. It was an ordinary day but then again not so, as I believe I will remember this for the rest of my life.

We have not always lived on Happy Street; there were many days, months, and maybe years, where the fights were dangerously destructive. I look back now and can see where we had to learn that giving in was our strength rather than a weakness.

My husband, an ordinary person, has been a civil servant for 30 years with the same municipality in the City of Baltimore. We came to each other in our early 30's with much baggage and three children between us. Both of us had been hurt deeply by the loss of a spouse through death.

The common ground was we are both Catholic, Italian, born in 1959 and from large families where there was more love than money. Brian was one of six children; I was one of five girls. Our core values were the same. I think he would agree, his family was city poor, having grown up in the inner city of Baltimore. I came from a farm in northeast Pennsylvania where we were poor yet the difference was I didn't know it the way he did.

One of the saddest stories my husband ever shared was also one which would play a huge role in defining him. His senior year in high school his lacrosse team lettered and he received his "S" letter for Southern High School. He said he was so proud. When he went home and asked his father for the money for the jacket, the response was, "We can't afford it." Brian was the only senior on the team without a jacket, and as a result was pushed to the end when the group photo was taken. In many ways his humiliation, it was a blessing – it pushed him hard to succeed. He is the only sibling who moved out of the city and escaped poverty. The curse is he never allows our kids to do without. His heart is in the right place, because he never wants our children to feel such hurt and humiliation.

What is your partner's story? How did it make you feel?

Adopted kids – you can love an adopted child as your own!

"You came upon me wave on wave." Country music artist Pat Green

I met my twins, a son and daughter when they were just 87 days old. Together their birth weight was less than my first born daughter. The twins were born 8-weeks pre-mature and their birth mother died from complications related to child birth.

I bonded with my older daughter during my pregnancy by singing and talking to her. From the moment I found out I was pregnant I didn't drink a drop of alcohol or smoke a single cigarette. Because of this intense bonding pre-birth I questioned adoptive mothers, it seemed they missed out. But I was to learn you can love an adopted child as your own. The love for my twins "came upon me wave on wave."

My younger daughter was so small, with a birth weight of just over 3 pounds and her twin brother was just over 5 pounds. They were infants when I met them and began the bonding process. Taking care of a tiny baby and helping them to grow came naturally. My husband, their natural father always promoted me as their mother.

Years later when my youngest daughter was a teenager she would share with me that one of her girlfriends asked her, "is that your step-mom?" Her response was, "no that's my mom!" It warmed my heart. I always raised the twins as my very own. As soon as they were old enough to understand we shared the story of their birth mother, "Angel Stacey" with them.

We still talk about it, "why did God decide to take their mother?" We don't know the answer but always come to the realization, we wouldn't be the family we have become if things didn't happen the way they did.

Share your thoughts

My Greatest Disappointment

The sad reality for me is that my greatest disappointment would also be where I would have wanted my greatest success. In 1998 just one month after high school graduation, my then 17 year old, would decide to move out of our home and never speak to me again. This would also be my greatest humiliation. She had graduated from prep school with all her college choices accepting her. She had a boyfriend, a car and a part-time job. On the outside she was a beautiful young woman voted by her classmates as most likely to be an attorney. Inside I knew she had been fractured by at least by two major losses/hurts. First, she would experience the sudden death of her father when she was just two. Five years later, at the age of seven, she would communicate to me that she had been abused at the hand of my mother's husband. This would cause me to lose my family as no one wanted to believe her. From the very beginning I chose to believe and support her. No regrets.

My daughter was my whole life. I took on each loss as a challenge that together we would overcome. Because she had these strikes against her, I pushed her even harder to succeed. I will never know her individual pain, but what I knew was I was determined that she would not lack in any way which I could help. My thoughts were that we could lie down and die or get up and live. Looking back I am certain I pushed her far too hard. My heart was right, my method, maybe, not so much.

I only wanted the best for her and I still do. When she left home, she was just a few months away from the age of eighteen and newly graduated from high school. In just a few days I would find her house keys and a "Dear Mom" letter she had dropped through our front door mail slot. It would state that she knew I wouldn't like her decisions but she had to go and to make them on her own. I decided it would be best if she returned on her own and not to go after her.

The next two weeks were completely void of any peace, where was she? How could I have meant so little to her? Didn't she miss me or love me at all? Miss her home and family, the twins?

Then I received a change of address verification (no new address) for her from the post office. I panicked. What if her boyfriend had hurt her? She could be dead somewhere for all I knew. I decided to call her beeper/cell phone, each time I would leave a message. I may have started out calm and concerned but as the time passed I was petrified and threatening. "If I don't hear from you I will have to call the police?" Then it would be if I don't hear from you at 1:00 then 3:00 then 6:00 I am calling the police. She never responded. I called my husband, we decided I needed to call the police she was still a minor and for all we knew she could be hurt or even worse.

I had no idea where she was staying; she had left the part-time job. She had shut down all her internet connections and our home phone never again rang for her.

The police came and I made a report. They said they would bring her home when they found her. It was the 4th of July and later that night they would call and say they had her. I needed to come to the police station. Here I was at the age of 38 and this would be my first visit ever to a police station. During the drive were so many thoughts, "why hadn't they brought her home like they said they would?" "Was she pregnant and afraid to tell me?" Nothing in my entire life could prepare me for what was ahead.

When I arrived, she was sitting in a chair and I could see she had been crying. I also witnessed for the very first time her disrespect for me as she rolled her eyes and looked away.

The police wouldn't let her go because she had told them I had abused her. I was certain I was going to vomit. How could she? At first I started to defend myself then I was like I'm out of here. If she was going to resort to this to declare her independence then just go!

That night our phone rang over and over and I was just frozen. Shock! I had calls telling me I had to report to the local courthouse the Monday after this weekend. I wanted to die I was completely humiliated! I had never been involved on either side of any court case. The police wouldn't let her go so I left and as a result they tried to charge me with abandonment. My friend, an attorney laughed out loud, he knew how ridiculous this was. I couldn't find the humor.

It would take a few social workers not long before it was declared "unfounded" but the damage was done. She had changed her story many times. First I was the abuser then my husband and then back to me. The twins she stated were, "very well cared for" and later when she was losing they too were abused. Whatever river was between us was now an ocean. She had taken up with a family, a cop and a barmaid at her boyfriend's friend's house. These people would take her in and shelter her. I tried to get a meeting with them and was denied. During the one and only phone conversation with the barmaid, she would ask me, "Can I ask you a question?" I said, "sure anything?" The only question she had, "how did you get our phone number?" I believe if I took in a troubled seventeen year old, I would at least check out the parents rather than garner all my information from the teenager. It would become clearer to me why my daughter was so enthralled with guns and getting gun certified since her "new family" included a cop.

I had experienced the death of my first husband and the loss of my family as a result of her abuse allegations, but nothing would compare to the pain her departure would cast on me. My skin hurt, I could barely breathe. I had no understanding. My daughter would hit me where it hurt most, in my mother's heart.

After much therapy and counseling I was making it day by day. More than a year would pass when I would learn she had a five-month old son. Any progress I had made was now gone. If she could go through an entire pregnancy and birth a baby and never reach out to me, she never would. This was almost more than I could bear. At the age of 23, her court papers would confirm she and the baby's father had signed over physical custody of their son to the cop and the barmaid.

67

In some sick way this was a small form of vindication, she had cast me away like garbage and now she had given her first born son away. Surely there was much more to her than just mother-daughter conflicts.

What I know for sure is my older daughter was slated for success under my care with a 4-year, $60,000 college scholarship awaiting her in an honors course of study. She had college credits before day one of college. Within months of her departure, and under the influence of her "new family," she would become a teen unwed mother.

It has been 11 years now since I have had my older daughter in my life, nothing will ever take her place or fill the void that she has left. I don't think I will ever "get over it" but I have learned how to live without her. There is not a day that goes by that I don't think of her.

The loss of my relationship with my older daughter is and will always be my greatest disappointment in life.

What is your greatest disappointment in life?

What really matters this Thanksgiving

At the time of this writing I have been parenting for just over 27 years, there have been many years when I believed my parenting skills to be in line with my life's greatest accomplishments and others when I just knew I totally missed the mark.

In parenting I learned love truly is blind, that letting go is by far the greatest challenge and seldom does it matter what I really want for my children. In the end it comes down to their life, their way.

I have loved and lost in parenting, to where my skin hurt and the hole left in my heart was at least the size of a cannonball. My kids taught me the true meaning of love, where you give and give and expect nothing in return. It is the only relationship where you literally bring that child, into the world and give them life. You give life to your child who may live in a way you may never understand, but you know the gift was in the giving.

With the three children I have mothered, I have learned each child is different and comes with their own likes, dislikes, talents and abilities. I have learned where environment may matter, it does not translate into the same environment, same outcome for each child.

I have learned humility in parenting and put myself in places and spaces I would never have gone without the hand holding of my child who lead me there. It was in parenting I learned that children have immediate needs and that the adults in my life could wait. It was my children that taught me patience and my children that taught me to trust in the letting go. My kids taught me all children lie at some point and not to take it personally or believe because your view is one of a close parent child relationship, it will mean honesty at all times, on all issues.

If the definition of forgiveness is letting go of how you thought it should be, then too it was my children that taught me to forgive. I learned to forgive myself before I could begin to forgive them, or any others. As amazing as giving birth is so is the circle of life, after 27 years of parenting I have learned much from my children and all the many enrichments they have afforded me. We are not finished parenting, as two of my children are in high school, and although they are currently doing well in most areas I have learned change will come. Changes will come with new driver's licenses, part time jobs, new friends, first loves, achievements and disappointments.

My children have collectively taught me most if not all the important lessons I have learned and this Thanksgiving it is my children and my husband that I am most thankful. (Originally published in The North County News and The Catholic Review)

What are you most thankful for?

Favorite Places of Mine …

Ft. Lauderdale, Florida
From the very first time I visited the beaches in Ft. Lauderdale I fell in love! The warmth of the sun coupled with the warm ocean water. I was fortunate to live there for a year in the early 1990's. In 1997 my husband and I married on the beach in Ft. Lauderdale. Key West is also a favorite place; there is a special energy to the buzz created on Duval Street.

Nashville, Tennessee
Several years ago I started travelling to Nashville for the country music scene. We love the Gaylord Opryland at Christmas, The Ryman Auditorium and downtown Nashville. It is a warm and inviting city and wonderful for country music fans like myself!

Allentown, Pennsylvania
Having grown up in and around Allentown I have fond memories of this city. Downtown used to be so wonderful when Hess's department store was there. Some of my favorite places to visit are the Farmer's Market, the Rose Garden, Yocco's for a hotdog and Josh Early for chocolate!

Lewes, Delaware
Our family spends a great deal of our off time in and around Lewes and Rehoboth beaches. Lewes is a quaint old town with a lot of history and boutique shopping. It's fun to take the ferry boat from Lewes to Cape May. Rehoboth is the beach area that we like for its charm, eateries and shopping. We spend many summer days on this beach.

Chicago, Illinois
Chicago is my favorite big city! The magnificent mile is just that – magnificent! The theater, shopping and the restaurant choices are outstanding. When I am there I feel energized and walk and walk and walk. There is a reason they are known for deep dish pizza, it's hard to have a favorite when there are so many excellent choices.

St Thomas, Virgin Island
Some of the most beautiful beaches, the color of the water is just amazing! It is a great place for shopping, a definite tourist attraction.

Lancaster, Pennsylvania
I am in awe of the Amish; the fact that they have maintained their lifestyle just amazes me. I love the countryside and all the farms. I enjoy people watching here.

Where do you travel, what are your favorite places to visit?

Make Something, Build Something, Grow Something

I love to bake! Cookies, cakes and pies represent for me, art that you eat. When I was a little girl my grandmother used to make pizzelle cookies (Italian waffle cookies) I loved the look of them as much as I enjoyed eating them. When I grew up I purchased my own pizzelle maker, such an easy cookie to make. I like anything baked and I enjoy just taking it in and admiring the finished product. For me, there is something about making something homemade that allows me to feel an immediate sense of accomplishment.

I have grown flowers and rose bushes and just last year I had success in growing a few perfect pumpkins. I felt like a mother of a newborn as I witnessed my pumpkins grow. I love to grow fresh basil and tomatoes, these simple pleasures help to refresh my soul.

Making dinner is still one of the small ways I show my love for my family. Most nights we still enjoy "the family table" at dinner time. I love making food for them to enjoy. It is the time of day when we all come together and compare stories from our day.

Making food allows me to nurture my family and celebrate the gifts of the season. There is nothing as special as fresh picked peaches or blueberries for a homemade pie. In the winter I love having the warmth of the oven, as I bake breads, cookies and cakes.

In 1997, my husband and I built a small beach home. For us it is like a child that together, we created. Taking something from one dimensional paper to a three dimensional completed house was very rewarding. Our family and friends have spent many years of happy memories there.

For me, there is nothing like the sense of accomplishment, created from making something, no matter how big or small.

What do you like to make or grow? What do you create that gives you a sense of accomplishment?

Papal Visit- he is a rock star!

In April of 2008 I was extremely fortunate to receive tickets for myself, my husband, and our twin teenagers to attend the Papal Mass in Washington. D.C. We were thrilled to be invited! We woke at 3:00 in the morning, drove to the D.C. metro, and arrived long before the large crowd. We secured our seats, and though it was hours away, took in every view, face and moment. This was the only day our kids missed a day of school. What better classroom? It was a cold morning and we were at Nationals Stadium in a covered area without sun. We shared stadium blankets and bonded as a family catching up on all the recent happenings in our lives.

I felt so blessed to work for the Archdiocese of Baltimore, where this type of an event is viewed as an extension of my work and life path. I was delighted to experience the event with my immediate family.

I had loved Pope John Paul II and still had some warming up to do to our newest Pope Benedict XVI. The stadium filled to maximum capacity. There was security every where and a continual parade of the most holy men and women of the cloth who had front and center floor seats. Watching the sisters, the priests and the parade of Cardinals held my attention. The procession was long but seemed like only minutes.

When the Pope arrived – the stadium went electric. I remember turning to my husband and saying "It's as though he's a rock star!" People were shouting "Father! Viva le Papa!" and openly praying. It was the only time I can remember being in a sports arena filled to the brim with love, hope, peace, joy, life, goodness, and yes, greatness! The most Holy, had come to us, the followers. The Pope spoke of abuse and expressed sorrow and acknowledgement of the hurt that had come from many in the church. This was a huge leap from the old school Catholics who lived in denial. The pontiff was soft spoken in a strangely strong manner; I was completely captivated. This event led me to learn more about this man, so I read several of his books and writings.

Pope Benedict had inspired me to go deeper in my faith, to learn more, to attempt to be a better Catholic, a better wife, and a better mother and friend. He is the Catholic equivalent to a rock star!

What event have you attended that moved you?

Dr. Ross, mentor and true visionary

"It is through the struggle that we find enlightenment." The Children's Guild was the perfect medicine at the perfect time. I had gone through a very painful loss in 1998, the year my daughter decided to amputate me from her life. Nothing had prepared me for this, I didn't see it coming. I thought she and I shared a binding love that would last forever. I could not have been more wrong.

From late 1998 to early 2000 I was lifeless, the walking wounded, and a body that moved yet had been completely gutted. During this time, I made business decisions that amounted to complete failure.

Things were bad. I decided to look for a job and stumbled upon a magical school called The Children's Guild. It is an innovative school for students, pre-school through high school, who have been traumatized, or are autistic, or who have multiple disabilities. It is filled with art, excites the senses and stimulates the intellect of children and youth others turn away from. The administration views these kids as gifted and talented, and helps them to learn, grow, and celebrate life through experiential education.

I was hired to manage special events and work in a school to work program, a program for teenagers who needed assistance with job skills and purposeful work. These kids were tough. Many had survived a variety of learning, physical and emotional disorders.

One day while exiting my car to walk inside the building, a police car was in the driveway. I watched as they escorted a kid half my size in hand cuffs. Another time I was conversing with a board member in the hallway when a student twice my size walked by and spit in my face. I didn't know this boy nor did he know me. I witnessed physical fights. The people that run this place are amazing, committed to helping these young people. They are talented teachers, social workers, artists, musicians, and actors.

It is in giving that we receive. I put myself out there. I worked hard, and threw myself into a new environment that was completely uncomfortable and foreign. I gained so much more than I could have imagined from this experience.

Not long after I was hired I garnered the attention of the president and CEO, Dr. Andrew Ross. A co-worker referred to him as a "visionary." It was true! This guy is amazing. He holds a PhD yet speaks like a regular guy and truly is one of the most humble people I have known. I learned so much from Andy; such as not to view failure as a negative, but to applaud the effort, at least you were trying. I've learned to view my past as the road to a sense of enlightenment because I had struggled so. He was one of the toughest bosses I've ever had, yet his strength was gentle. He expected much if you were to work along side of him.

I learned a lot at The Children's Guild that served me well in my career. Andy doesn't teach religion yet his principals could easily coincide with my religious training. He doesn't discriminate he sees the good in people and in doing so, pulls the best out of them. I am, and will always be grateful for my years at The Children's Guild. The people who work there are doing God's work.

Find great mentors and do your best to keep those relationships alive.

Another mentor named Marianne

She was a southern belle and a socialite and would become my real estate manager. At just 26 years old, she would take me under her wing and help me to become one of the top 25% of the agents in my office in sales and listings. In my first year I would purchase my first home as a single parent.

Marianne was so upbeat and positive; she had such a high opinion of you that you never wanted to let her down. This was a huge contrast to the critical guilt laden Italian Catholic upbringing I had experienced. I found it so refreshing and motivating. It also brought me back to "if you think you can, you can!"

Real estate was loaded with practical knowledge. You learned about finance, mortgage rates, and programs; you learned about home construction, decorating, and landscaping. You knew who was moving out of state, who was being promoted, and who lost their job. You knew who retired, who newly married, who passed away, and who needed a bigger home to accommodate a growing family. You learned about neighborhoods and lifestyles, and ultimately, about contracts and negotiations. Real estate taught me about property values, neighborhoods, and people's lifestyles. I learned money doesn't necessarily buy good taste, or cleanliness.

I learned that for many people, their home represented social status; others, the American dream. I learned some houses were homes; others simply houses. I learned at the end of the day, a house was just bricks and sticks.

I had been to settlement with people who could pay cash for a house; and others who had the U-haul loaded outside, thrilled to have barely avoided foreclosure. I sold and listed properties in dangerous neighborhoods and the wealthiest. I learned about condos and farms, developed and undeveloped land. The greatest gift would be the transferable skills that would help me "close the deal" in future endeavors.

The network of people I met would aid me in all my work after the real estate career ended.

Who has mentored you? What traits have you adopted from them?

Working for a Priest – Fr. Marty

Now this was going to be different! Not only is my new supervisor a Catholic Priest, but it would be the very first time my supervisor would be younger than me. In the past, as a Catholic school girl I had a certain fear of Priests. The ones I knew seemed stern and standoffish, a bit scary.

Moments after we met we would discover we were both born in the same Catholic hospital in Hazleton, Pennsylvania. We also discovered we were both Italian and had mothers who were registered nurses.

Working at a youth retreat house I would not only work for a Catholic Priest but by extension become friendly with many other Priests. One of the greatest gifts of the retreat house is the young Priests (some are young in age, some in spirit and most in both age and spirit) who come out and work with and support the youth.

Fr. Marty is the iron fist in the velvet glove, a soft spoken man with strength of conviction. He is a humble man who seldom, if at all, touts his success and accomplishments. The advice given to me early on in working with a Priest was "he will be protected by the collar, when there is a conflict they will come after you." In this working relationship I always know he is my supervisor and that I would have to take the hit if necessary. In some ways I have had to be more disliked than I may normally have chosen to be.

Priests are held to a higher standard, they are trained to see "the face of God in every person" yet they are human. As an Administrator Fr. Marty wants what is best for the retreat house and all the youth The House serves. Many times there is conflict when his leadership wants to effect positive change in the culture. Many times he has been met with, "this is how we have always done it." Watching him weigh the conflicts and choosing his battles has been a lesson in itself. Even a Priest has to do battle at times!

In many ways I feel blessed to work with Fr. Marty but also in the environment here at the retreat house. It is such a special place.

Who are your mentors and what have they meant to you?

Death

I am scared to death to die! There, I said it! The best response I had to that statement came from my husband Brian. He said, "That's because you are not ready to die. When your time comes you will want to go because you are tired and it is your time." I felt a certain sense of calmness with those words. I immediately thought about one of my favorite childhood books, *Charlotte's Web*. To this day I love that story.

Remember the song by Queen the line that goes, "I don't want to die; sometimes I wish I was never born at all." The only time I feel like that is when I think about my fear of dying. Everything matters to me. I live a passionate life. I have been very fortunate to have loved all the work I have done and when I stopped loving it, I was able to move onto something else that I loved.

My first husband died when I was just 23, I have lost friends in their 20's, 30's and 40's to death. My sense was I would experience these losses because it was so hard for me to understand. I am a person of faith, but even scientifically speaking how does all that energy cease and die? Become nothing? Surely it has to go somewhere and become something else?

When my first husband died I read everything on death all Helen Kubler-Ross on Death and Dying, Leo Basagalia, Freddie the Leaf. Twelve years ago I wrote *Angel Stacey* to share our family story about death.

Everyone has a story. For me I have an ordinary life. Take the ordinary things and make them extraordinary. Life is for the living – live it!

I have accepted that because I love life, I fear death. I want to live and experience it all. Maybe someday I will be ready to go but not now. This year I will turn 50, and hopefully I am only Halfway Home.

No one wants to talk about death? But we will all experience it and the loss of others close to us? Share your feelings and stories?

My Dream for the future

My dream for my later years has been the same dream I have always dreamt. I see myself with my husband and our Bichon living on the beach, a big house in a small resort town like Bethany Beach, Delaware. The house has full floor to ceiling windows off the kitchen and living areas and the living room has a spiral staircase that takes you right to the sandy beach. We decorate in comfy French Country.

We chose Bethany over Florida beaches for the changing of the seasons. In the winter months we are casual and drink fine wine, cook fresh meats, seafood and vegetables and appreciate the warmth of a crackling fire. There are few neighbors year round and we run the beach with our dog and enjoy the solitude. This is the season I write my novels. My husband lives for the dog and me and probably in that order!

When spring and summer arrive, my husband is my agent and we travel promoting my recent book. During these months we are very social and completely manicured a complete contrast from how we live during the fall and winter months. After months of travel and being on the road we return home for another fall and winter at the beach. Our down time is full of art and writing and an appreciation of the close relationship we share. I do sense that we may have to win the lottery first, that is also part of my dream!

Our kids are well and we have peace and enjoy them and our grandchildren. We have friends who visit and stay awhile and others we meet up with during our travel. We are healthy and happy. Life is good!

What dreams do you have for the future?

My Heaven

How do you imagine Heaven? What does it look like? Who is there?

For me Heaven looks like white fluffy clouds and everyone is wearing white cotton clothes. God our Father is there and welcomes us. We meet up with all the people from our past life and new acquaintances. There is no crime or violence in Heaven; there are no starving people and no such thing as poor or underprivileged. There is peace and comfort; there are no worries about paying taxes, mortgages and raising kids. There is no such thing as air pollution and global warming. Either all our questions are answered or it becomes clear they were all irrelevant to begin with.

In Heaven there is warmth with cool fresh air and people pray and speak quietly and calmly. It is a clean place where love roots all things. In Heaven, we have the ability to look down on life without judgment. There is no hatred, anger, jealousy, disrespect or hurt.

There is abundance in Heaven without any overindulgence. In Heaven, we are assigned tasks that fit our souls; some will be angels, the messengers of God. In Heaven, we float in our lightness of being. Heaven rights all our wrongs.

"Every body wants to go to heaven, just not right now." Country music artist Kenny Chesney

What's your Heaven?

A favorite of mine

Comes the Dawn

After a while you learn the subtle difference
between holding a hand and chaining a soul
and you learn that love doesn't mean leaning
and company doesn't mean security

and you begin to understand that kisses aren't contracts
and presents aren't promises
and you begin to accept your defeats
with head held high and your eyes wide open

with the grace of a woman, not the grief of a child
you learn to build your roads
on today because tomorrow's ground
is too uncertain for plans, and futures have

a way of falling down in mid-flight
after a while you learn that even sunshine
burns if you get too much
so you plant your own garden and decorate

your own soul, instead of waiting
for someone to bring you flowers
and you learn that you really can endure,
that you really are strong

and you really have worth
and you learn and learn, and you learn

with every goodbye you learn

~author unknown~

Write your favorites here

Another favorite

People are often unreasonable and self-centered.
FORGIVE THEM ANYWAY.

If you are kind, people may accuse you of ulterior motives.
BE KIND ANYWAY.

If you are honest, people may cheat you.
BE HONEST ANYWAY.

If you find happiness, people may be jealous.
BE HAPPY ANYWAY.

The good you do today may be forgotten tomorrow.
DO GOOD ANYWAY.

Give the world the best you have, and it may never be enough.
GIVE YOUR BEST ANYWAY.

For you see, in the end, it is between you and God.
IT NEVER WAS BETWEEN YOU AND THEM ANYWAY.

~Mother Teresa~

Write your favorites here

Meet Bernadette …

Bernadette Moyer resides in Lutherville, Maryland, along with her husband Brian Sahm and their twin teenagers, a son and a daughter. During most holidays, summer vacations and off time you will find them at their second home in Lewes, Delaware. Her oldest daughter is twenty-eight and lives on her own. Bernadette was widowed at the age of twenty-three and it was the death of her first husband that taught her the true value of life – "Life is for the living, live it!" She will turn fifty this year and that milestone is one of the reasons for sharing her stories.

Bernadette is the author of *Angel Stacey* (a children's book on parents turned angels) she has written for *Surviving Ophelia* and has several published articles to her credit.

Currently Bernadette serves as the Director of Development for The Archdiocese of Baltimore's Monsignor O'Dwyer Retreat House in Sparks, Maryland. You can e-mail her at bmoyer@archbalt.org or bmoyer37@aol.com.

"Each and every time I finish writing a book, I feel as though I have given birth to a new baby. I truly hope you will enjoy *Halfway Home,* my newest offspring."

For additional book purchases;

Books can be purchased at amazon.com or directly through the retreat house by e-mailing bmoyer@archbalt.org or bmoyer37@aol.com or mail request to:

Bernadette A. Moyer
c/o Msgr. O'Dwyer Retreat House
15523 York, Road
Sparks Maryland 21152

Books purchased through the retreat house are discounted 25% or $15.each, with additional cost of $3.95 for shipping & handling

Bulk Order Discount
6 -11 copies - $12.00 each
12 -18 copies - $10.00 each

Please note all books purchased benefit The Founders Youth Recreational Facility Capital Campaign at The Msgr. O'Dwyer Retreat House located in Sparks, Maryland.

For retreat house information, visit our website at www.msgrodwyer.org